Flex Revolution: Redefining the Future of Work

Frederique Bergeron

All rights reserved.

ISBN: 9798340048837

CONTENTS

1	The Evolution of Remote Work	2
2	Why Flexibility is the Future of Work	5
3	The Regressive Push for Return to Office	9
4	Women and Flexibility—A Disproportionate Burden	13
5	Work-Life Integration vs. Work-Life Balance	16
6	Digital Fatigue and the New Workday Structure	19
7	Managing Distributed Teams Across Time Zones	22
8	The Hybrid Work Model—Balancing Remote and In-Office Work	25
9	The Role of HR in Supporting Flexibility	29
10	Remote Work and Career Development	33
11	New Perspectives—Older Employees, Gen Z, and Digital Nomads	37
12	Trust vs. Surveillance—The Battle for Remote Work Autonomy	40
13	Legal and Compliance Challenges in Remote Work	42
14	The Future of Office Spaces—From Desks to Collaboration Hubs	45
15	Remote Work and Environmental Sustainability	49
16	Building a Strong Employee Experience in Remote Teams	51
17	The Future of Work for Front-Line Workers: Bridging the Divide	54
18	Rethinking Office Space in a Remote-First World	59
19	Resilience and Adaptability—Key Competencies for Remote Work	65

INTRODUCTION: THE FUTURE OF WORK IS FLEXIBLE

The world of work is changing faster than ever. In the past few decades, we've seen gradual shifts toward flexible work, but the COVID-19 pandemic pushed it into overdrive. What started as a temporary solution has now become a permanent fixture in many organizations. Remote work, flexible hours, and the merging of personal and professional life are no longer the exception—they are becoming the norm.

But this shift is not just about technology or necessity. It's about humanity. The traditional 9-to-5 workweek, rigid office schedules, and the expectation of constant physical presence no longer align with how people live their lives today. A flexible approach is the cornerstone of shaping a future workplace that truly prioritizes people and their well-being. It offers employees the autonomy to balance their professional responsibilities with personal needs and allows companies to tap into a more engaged, productive workforce.

This book will explore how organizations can embrace flexibility, overcome the challenges of remote work, and create a work environment that prioritizes well-being without sacrificing results. Whether you're an HR professional, a manager, or an employee navigating the new world of work, this book is for you. Together, we'll unpack the reasons why flexibility is the future and how you can help create a more humane workplace.

1 THE EVOLUTION OF REMOTE WORK

A Brief History of Work: From the Industrial Revolution to the Digital Age

The concept of work as we know it today has undergone massive transformations over centuries. Before the Industrial Revolution, most people worked in agrarian settings—farms, workshops, or family-owned businesses. Work was often seasonal and integrated with daily life. The rise of factories in the late 18th and 19th centuries, however, fundamentally changed this.

The Industrial Revolution: The Birth of the 9-to-5

During the Industrial Revolution, factory owners needed large groups of workers to be in the same place at the same time. This shift brought about the concept of fixed working hours, which eventually led to the standardization of the 9-to-5 workday. Workers clocked in and out, and productivity was directly tied to time spent in the factory.

This rigid schedule became the blueprint for most modern jobs, even as industries moved away from manufacturing to more office-based work. The idea that workers must be physically present and working for a set number of hours each day persisted, even as technology began to create new possibilities for flexibility.

The Office Era: The 20th Century

As the world industrialized further, office work became the new frontier. White-collar jobs in administration, finance, and communication replaced factory jobs for a significant portion of the workforce. The rise of skyscrapers in cities like New York and London created massive office spaces, where employees would gather to complete their tasks under the watchful eyes of managers.

For decades, this office-centric model persisted. The tools of the trade evolved from typewriters and filing cabinets to computers and email, but the idea of "going to work" at a physical location remained a constant.

The Information Age: Work Begins to Shift

By the late 20th century, advances in technology began to disrupt traditional work structures. The internet, email, and mobile phones allowed work to be done outside of the office for the first time. While most companies still required employees to be physically present, the seeds of remote work had been planted.

Companies like IBM were early adopters of telecommuting in the 1980s, allowing select employees to work from home as a cost-saving measure. However, widespread remote work was still decades away.

The Digital Age: Remote Work Takes Hold

The 21st century brought rapid advancements in technology, including high-speed internet, cloud computing, and video conferencing tools like Zoom and Skype. These technologies enabled employees to work from virtually anywhere, but the office remained the dominant workspace—until the COVID-19 pandemic.

The pandemic forced companies worldwide to adopt remote work en masse. What was once a temporary solution has now become a permanent fixture in many industries, leading to the widespread acceptance of flexible work models that combine remote, hybrid, and office-based work.

This historical progression shows that work structures have always evolved in response to technological and societal changes, and remote work is the next step in that long evolution.

The Early Days of Telecommuting

Remote work might seem like a recent trend, but the idea has been around for decades. In the 1970s, as computers became more common in offices, some forward-thinking companies began experimenting with telecommuting. The idea was simple: employees could work from home using telephones and early computers to stay connected to their offices.

These early telecommuters were often people with highly specialized roles that didn't require their constant presence in the office. The technology was limited, and most companies were hesitant to embrace the idea. The model of success at the time was rooted in physical presence—being seen by managers and colleagues meant you were working.

The Impact of Technology

As technology advanced, so did the potential for remote work. The rise of the internet in the 1990s, followed by the mass adoption of smartphones, laptops, and cloud computing in the 2000s, made remote work far more accessible. Employees could now collaborate on projects from different locations, communicate via email, and share documents in real-time.

Despite the availability of these tools, remote work remained the exception rather than the rule. Most companies were still wedded to the idea of physical offices as the hub of productivity and collaboration. However, a few early adopters, like Automattic (the company behind WordPress) and Basecamp, built remote-first businesses, proving that it was possible to thrive without traditional office spaces.

The Pandemic and Remote Work

The COVID-19 pandemic changed everything. Practically overnight, companies worldwide were forced to send their employees home and embrace remote work on an unprecedented scale. What was initially seen as a temporary solution became a long-term reality. Many organizations discovered that not only could their teams work remotely, but they could do so with increased productivity, better work-life balance, and reduced costs.

2 WHY FLEXIBILITY IS THE FUTURE OF WORK

Flexibility as a Productivity Booster

One of the biggest lessons from the shift to remote work is that flexibility leads to better outcomes. When employees are given the freedom to manage their own schedules, they are often more productive, creative, and engaged. This is because flexibility allows employees to work during their peak hours and take breaks when they need them, without the rigid structure of a traditional 9-to-5 schedule.

Studies have shown that flexible work arrangements reduce burnout and increase job satisfaction. Employees with control over their schedules can better manage personal responsibilities—whether that's picking up a child from school, running errands, or simply taking a walk to clear their minds. This freedom creates a more balanced work-life integration, leading to happier employees who perform better at their jobs.

The Business Case for Flexibility

Flexibility doesn't just benefit employees—it's good for business. Organizations that embrace flexible work policies see improved retention, reduced absenteeism, and increased engagement. Flexibility is also a key factor in attracting top talent. As more companies adopt remote work, employees have more options than ever. If your company doesn't offer flexibility, you risk losing talented workers to competitors who do.

Additionally, flexible work arrangements can significantly reduce overhead costs. By allowing employees to work remotely or in hybrid setups, companies can downsize their office spaces, reduce utilities, and save on amenities like food, parking, and transit subsidies.

Automattic: Leading the Charge with a Fully Remote Workforce

Automattic, the company behind WordPress, has been a fully distributed company for years. With over 1,200 employees across 77 countries, Automattic has developed a sophisticated approach to remote work. They've created a culture that prioritizes communication and results over physical presence. Automattic's tools, like P2 (their internal collaboration tool), are designed to foster asynchronous communication, making it easier for global teams to collaborate without the need for constant meetings.

Automattic's success in maintaining a highly productive and collaborative remote workforce has set a benchmark for the tech industry, proving that distributed teams can work efficiently across different time zones with the right tools and culture in place.

Key Takeaway: The tech sector, with its focus on innovation and digital solutions, was one of the first to embrace remote work at scale. Companies like Automattic show that success in remote work hinges on building strong communication frameworks and maintaining a results-oriented mindset.

Global Perspectives on Flexibility: A Worldwide Shift

While remote and flexible work is a growing trend globally, different countries and regions have adopted these practices at different paces. In many ways, a nation's approach to work-life balance reflects its broader cultural values and labor laws. Let's explore how various countries have embraced flexible work arrangements and what the rest of the world can learn from their approaches.

The Netherlands: A Pioneer of Remote Work

The Netherlands has long been at the forefront of embracing flexible work arrangements. The Dutch workforce is known for its high levels of autonomy and a strong emphasis on work-life balance. Even before the pandemic, the Dutch government passed laws making it easier for employees to request flexible work hours or remote work arrangements, and employers are legally required to consider these requests.

In the Netherlands, there is a cultural acceptance of remote work, with many employees splitting their time between home and the office. This flexibility is supported by progressive labor laws that prioritize the well-being of employees, recognizing that work can be completed just as effectively outside of the office.

Germany: Emphasizing Employee Rights

Germany, like the Netherlands, has long been a leader in labor rights and work-life balance. Germany's strong labor unions have pushed for policies that promote flexibility, such as reduced work hours, remote work, and comprehensive parental leave. Many German companies adopted hybrid models early, allowing workers to be productive both in the office and at home.

A particularly interesting policy is Germany's **"Right to Disconnect"**, which grants employees the right to ignore work-related communications outside of office hours, ensuring that flexibility doesn't lead to burnout. This protects employees' personal time and supports healthier work-life boundaries.

Finland: Experimenting with a Shorter Workweek

Finland has long been at the cutting edge of innovative labor policies. One of the most notable examples is Finland's trial of a four-day workweek and six-hour workdays. This experiment was designed to promote work-life balance, reduce stress, and increase productivity. Finland's focus on flexibility extends beyond remote work—it reimagines the very structure of the workweek, emphasizing efficiency over time spent at a desk.

United States and Canada: Flexibility as a Competitive Advantage

North American companies, particularly in the United States and Canada, have been slower to adopt government-mandated flexible work policies. However, tech companies and startups in these regions were some of the first to adopt remote work as a standard practice. For many companies, offering flexibility became a competitive advantage in attracting and retaining top talent.

In the U.S., flexibility is often seen as a perk rather than a right, and it's more prevalent in knowledge-based industries like tech and finance. The Canadian government, on the other hand, has started to explore policies that would support flexible work more broadly, especially as remote work has proven successful during the pandemic.

Asia: Embracing Flexibility Slowly

In many Asian countries, there has traditionally been a strong emphasis on physical presence and long working hours. Countries like Japan and South Korea are known for their "presenteeism" culture, where employees are expected to be in the office for long hours, regardless of productivity. However, the pandemic forced many companies in Asia to adopt remote work, and there are early signs that this could lead to more flexible work practices in the future.

China, while a major player in the global workforce, has also seen a slower adoption of remote work. In many Chinese companies, face-to-face collaboration is still highly valued, though the pandemic has spurred interest in hybrid models.

Work-Life Integration: A New Paradigm

For decades, we've talked about work-life balance as the ideal—striking the perfect equilibrium between professional and personal responsibilities. But in the age of remote work, a new paradigm is emerging: work-life integration. Instead of rigidly separating work and life, work-life integration allows the two to coexist fluidly. It acknowledges that personal tasks might need to happen during the workday and that work tasks might extend into evenings or weekends.

This approach is more realistic for the modern workforce, especially as people juggle multiple roles at home and work. By embracing work-life integration, companies can create a more supportive environment where employees can manage both their personal lives and their careers without sacrificing one for the other.

3 THE REGRESSIVE PUSH FOR RETURN TO OFFICE

Ditching Outdated Office Mandates

Despite the clear and well-documented benefits of remote work, many companies continue to push for employees to return to the office. The reasons given are often outdated and rooted in traditional management beliefs: the need for collaboration, preserving office culture, or the notion that productivity happens best in person. However, in a post-pandemic world with advanced technology and changing employee expectations, these reasons are increasingly coming under scrutiny.

1. The Collaboration Myth

In the past, offices were seen as essential spaces for collaboration. Physical proximity was viewed as the key to teamwork, creativity, and problem-solving. However, this notion is now largely obsolete. Today, with the rise of sophisticated digital tools, collaboration can happen seamlessly regardless of physical location. Tools like Slack, Microsoft Teams, Zoom, and Asana allow teams to communicate, brainstorm, and manage projects in real-time across the globe.

The argument that innovation and collaboration suffer when employees work remotely simply doesn't hold up anymore. Many companies have reported that remote work has not only maintained but, in some cases, increased collaboration. By offering flexible work environments, employees feel empowered, creative, and connected. The idea that the office is the only place where collaboration thrives is based on an outdated understanding of how work is conducted in the modern era.

2. Preserving Office Culture

Another commonly cited reason for pushing a return to the office is to preserve or strengthen company culture. While it is true that in-person interactions can help build relationships, the belief that office culture only flourishes in a physical space overlooks the opportunity to build a new kind of culture—one that is inclusive, flexible, and adaptive to a global workforce.

A strong company culture isn't about how often people are in the office but about how connected they feel to their colleagues and the company's mission. Remote-first companies like GitLab and Automattic have built thriving, values-driven cultures without any physical office presence, proving that company culture can evolve to meet the demands of a distributed workforce.

The Absurdity of In-Office Virtual Meetings

One of the most frustrating and illogical outcomes of the return-to-office push is the rise of in-office virtual meetings. Employees are commuting long distances, rearranging their lives, and spending time and money just to sit at a desk in the office and join video calls with colleagues who are still working remotely.

This creates a bizarre scenario where employees are forced to leave the comfort and convenience of their home offices only to spend their entire day interacting virtually. The question must be asked: if the meetings are virtual, why should it matter where the employees attend them from? The inefficiency of this practice is glaring, and it highlights the disconnect between management's desire to have people physically present and the reality of how work is actually getting done.

Examples of Companies Facing Pushback

There are numerous examples of companies attempting to bring employees back to the office, only to face significant pushback. Apple faced internal resistance when it announced that workers had to return to the office for a few days each week. Employees argued that the forced return was unnecessary and undermined the productivity and flexibility they had achieved remotely. Similarly, companies like Google and Amazon have grappled with reconciling employee demand for remote work with management's push for in-office presence.

Financial and Environmental Costs of Commuting

The financial and environmental implications of the return to office are another reason why this push is seen as regressive. For many workers, commuting is one of the most time-consuming and costly parts of their day. In cities with long commute times and expensive transportation options, employees are once again burdened with the high costs of gas, parking, public transportation, and lost time.

1. The Economic Toll

Commuting not only impacts employees' wallets but also their work-life balance. The time spent on the road or in public transport is time lost to personal pursuits, family, and rest. The added costs of commuting—especially in an era of rising fuel prices—can significantly affect an employee's financial well-being. Remote work has proven to alleviate this strain, allowing employees to save money and spend more time on activities that enhance their quality of life.

2. Environmental Impact

Returning to the office also comes with environmental consequences. The mass return to commuting increases carbon emissions, traffic congestion, and pollution. During the pandemic, when large numbers of employees worked from home, there was a significant reduction in carbon footprints. According to data from Global Carbon Project, CO_2 emissions dropped by an estimated 6.4% in 2020, largely due to decreased transportation and industrial activity.

For companies that claim to prioritize sustainability and environmental responsibility, the return to the office contradicts these values. Allowing employees to continue working remotely or in hybrid models not only supports their well-being but also significantly reduces the environmental impact, including carbon emissions and pollution. Insisting on in-office work may undermine corporate sustainability efforts and set back broader environmental progress.

Employee Well-Being and the Flexibility Demand

At the heart of the pushback against returning to the office is the issue of employee well-being. Over the past few years, employees have experienced the benefits of remote work—better work-life balance, reduced stress, and the ability to manage personal and professional responsibilities without the rigid confines of office life. The return to the office not only threatens to take away these benefits but also signals a lack of trust from management.

Surveys from sources like Gallup and McKinsey consistently show that employees value flexibility and are willing to leave companies that don't offer it. Flexibility has become a top priority, particularly for younger generations like Millennials and Gen Z, who are demanding more control over their time and location of work. Companies that fail to acknowledge this shift risk alienating their workforce and losing talent to more flexible competitors.

Conclusion: The Case for Evolving, Not Regressing

The regressive push to return to the office ignores the lessons learned over the past few years. Technology has evolved, work culture has shifted, and employees have adapted to a more flexible and productive way of working. The office as the central hub of work is no longer a necessity, and clinging to this outdated model risks alienating employees and harming both organizational efficiency and employee well-being.

Companies that embrace the future of flexible work will not only thrive in a competitive talent market but will also be better positioned to foster a culture of innovation, inclusivity, and sustainability. The question isn't why companies should allow remote work—it's why, in the face of all the evidence, some are so determined to return to the past.

4 WOMEN & FLEXIBILITY – A DISPROPORTIONATE BURDEN

The Pandemic's Impact on Women

The COVID-19 pandemic exposed and intensified the existing inequalities women face in the workforce. As schools and daycares closed, women were often the ones who took on the bulk of childcare and homeschooling responsibilities, leading many to reduce their working hours or leave their jobs altogether. The pandemic highlighted the double burden of unpaid domestic work and paid employment that women disproportionately shoulder, a problem that has persisted for decades.

This burden is even more pronounced for single mothers and caregivers of elderly or disabled family members. When workplaces fail to offer flexibility, it leaves women with impossible choices: continue working and sacrifice their family responsibilities, or step back from their careers, often at the cost of their financial independence and career progression.

Return-to-Office Mandates and Their Impact on Women

As companies push employees to return to the office, the brunt of this burden is once again falling on women. Many of the responsibilities that women took on during the pandemic haven't disappeared—children still need to be cared for, and households still need to be managed. Forcing women back into rigid office hours adds an unnecessary layer of stress, especially when remote work has already proven that it's possible to manage both personal and professional tasks effectively.

Furthermore, returning to the office often means commuting long distances and spending money on childcare, which disproportionately affects women in lower-wage jobs. Many women face the added pressure of maintaining the appearance of work-life balance while struggling with burnout from juggling both spheres.

Sarah, a senior manager in a tech firm, was able to manage her career and family during the pandemic thanks to her company's flexible work policies.

She explains:

"I'm a single mom, and remote work has been a lifeline for me. Before, I was constantly stressed about making it home in time for dinner or missing school events. Now, I can structure my day around my kids' needs and still meet my work deadlines. It's allowed me to be fully present both at home and at work."

Sarah's story reflects the broader impact of flexibility on women, particularly those with caregiving responsibilities. Remote work has allowed her to excel in her role while being there for her family. The flexibility Sarah experienced represents how such policies can bridge the gap for many women, allowing them to advance in their careers without sacrificing their family responsibilities.

How Flexibility Can Close the Gender Gap

Flexible work policies are a powerful tool for addressing gender inequality in the workplace. When women are given the freedom to manage their own schedules, they can balance family and career responsibilities without having to sacrifice one for the other. Remote work, hybrid models, and flexible hours allow women to remain engaged in the workforce while meeting the demands of home life.

For companies serious about promoting gender equity, flexibility should be a central part of their diversity, equity, and inclusion (DEI) strategy. By offering flexible work arrangements, companies can retain top female talent, reduce turnover, and create a more inclusive workplace where all employees—regardless of their caregiving responsibilities—can thrive.

Case Studies: Companies Supporting Women with Flexibility

- **Salesforce**: Salesforce has embraced flexible work by allowing employees to work from home most of the time. The company offers generous family leave policies and support for parents and caregivers, recognizing that flexibility is key to maintaining a diverse and inclusive workforce.

- **Vodafone:** Vodafone launched a global policy offering flexible work hours and the option for employees to work remotely. This policy has been particularly beneficial for women in caregiving roles, allowing them to manage their professional and personal responsibilities without compromising their careers.

5 WORK-LIFE INTEGRATION VS WORK-LIFE BALANCE

The Old Paradigm: Work-Life Balance

For years, the term "work-life balance" has been the ideal that employees and employers strive for—a clear division between work hours and personal time. The idea was that employees should be able to "switch off" after a certain time and fully engage with their personal lives. But in practice, this often created an artificial separation that didn't account for the complexities of real life.

For many people, personal responsibilities don't fit neatly into the hours outside of 9-to-5. Children need to be picked up from school, doctor's appointments happen during the day, and sometimes, a moment to do laundry or run an errand can make the rest of the workday more productive.

The New Paradigm: Work-Life Integration

Work-life integration acknowledges that the boundaries between personal and professional life are often fluid. Instead of rigidly separating the two, work-life integration allows for a more natural blend. Employees are trusted to manage their time and responsibilities, which means they can run personal errands during the day, attend important family events, and still get their work done—often more efficiently than before.

This approach allows employees to structure their day around their personal and professional obligations in a way that makes sense for them. It also recognizes that personal well-being is integral to professional success. When employees feel they can meet both personal and work responsibilities without guilt, they are more engaged and productive.

Cultural Impacts: Shifting to a Flexible Work Culture

The move from a traditional office-centric model to a flexible work environment isn't just a structural change—it requires a fundamental transformation of organizational culture. Flexibility is more than allowing employees to work remotely or offering hybrid schedules. It's about fostering a work environment that values autonomy, trust, and results over rigid adherence to office hours and physical presence.

Trust-Based Culture

To successfully embrace flexibility, companies need to move away from the "clock-in, clock-out" mentality and build a culture rooted in trust. In a flexible work environment, employees must be trusted to manage their time and responsibilities without micromanagement. This shift demands a cultural change, particularly in organizations where productivity has long been equated with physical presence.

- **Empowering Employees**: Organizations that thrive in flexible work environments empower employees to make decisions about how and when they work. This requires trust, clear communication, and a focus on outcomes rather than hours worked.
- **Leadership's Role**: Leaders play a pivotal role in modeling this shift. If leadership demonstrates flexibility and supports autonomy, it sets the tone for the entire organization. Managers who lead with trust inspire greater engagement and loyalty from their teams.

Fostering Communication and Inclusivity

A flexible work culture must also focus on open communication and inclusivity. Remote and hybrid workers need to feel just as connected and engaged as their in-office counterparts. Companies need to invest in technology that enables seamless communication and collaboration, while also promoting a culture that values all voices, regardless of location.

- **Virtual Watercooler Moments**: Cultural cohesion can suffer if remote employees feel isolated. HR should foster ways to create virtual spaces for informal communication, allowing employees to build relationships and share ideas in a less formal, non-task-oriented setting.

By building a culture that embraces flexibility, organizations not only increase productivity but also foster employee satisfaction and retention.

Trusting Employees to Manage Their Time

One of the keys to successful work-life integration is trust. Companies must move away from the outdated notion that employees need to be constantly monitored to ensure they're working. Micromanagement erodes trust and sends the message that employees are only valued for the hours they clock in, not the results they deliver.

In a results-oriented workplace, what matters is the outcome, not the specific hours worked. If an employee needs to step away for an hour to pick up their child or go to a doctor's appointment, it shouldn't be the company's business, as long as the work is done. This level of trust empowers employees to take ownership of their schedules and responsibilities, leading to higher job satisfaction and better performance.

Case Studies: Companies Embracing Work-Life Integration

- **Buffer**: Buffer is a remote-first company that allows employees to set their own schedules. The company emphasizes results over time spent at a desk, and employees are encouraged to integrate personal and professional tasks throughout their day.

- **Dropbox**: Dropbox adopted a "virtual first" work model, where employees can work from anywhere, and work-life integration is a core value. The company trusts its employees to manage their time and emphasizes flexibility as a key to productivity and well-being.

6 DIGITAL FATIGUE & THE NEW WORKDAY STRUCTURE

The Rise of Digital Fatigue

With the shift to remote work came an unexpected consequence: digital fatigue. Virtual meetings, once an occasional event, quickly became the norm. Employees found themselves spending hours each day on video calls, often with little time in between. The convenience of tools like Zoom, Microsoft Teams, and Slack made it easy to stay connected, but it also blurred the lines between work and rest.

Digital fatigue sets in when employees feel overwhelmed by the constant demand for virtual communication. The mental energy required to stay engaged in back-to-back video calls is far greater than that required for in-person meetings. As a result, many employees are experiencing burnout, even as they work from the comfort of their own homes.

Challenges of Flexibility: Managing Burnout in a Flexible World

While flexibility offers significant benefits, it also poses unique challenges, particularly around burnout. The flexibility that enables employees to work from home or outside traditional hours can make it harder to maintain a clear separation between work and personal life. This "always on" culture can lead to digital fatigue, burnout, and reduced productivity.

- **Establishing Boundaries**: One of the major challenges of remote work is that the home can become an extension of the office, making it difficult for employees to fully disconnect. HR can address this by setting guidelines that encourage employees to log off during non-working hours and take regular breaks throughout the day.
- **Over-Communication**: With virtual meetings and communication tools like Slack or Teams, employees can feel overwhelmed by the constant flow of information. HR can recommend strategies such as "meeting-free days" or encouraging asynchronous

communication to give employees more control over their schedules and prevent burnout.

- **Mental Health Resources**: To combat burnout, HR should promote mental health initiatives, including access to counseling, wellness programs, and mental health days. Flexibility must extend beyond working hours to support employees' overall well-being.

By acknowledging the potential challenges of flexibility, HR can create a more balanced work environment that promotes both productivity and enhance employees' quality of life.

Rethinking the Workday to Combat Fatigue

To combat digital fatigue, companies need to rethink how they structure the workday. It's not enough to simply move the traditional office schedule online; instead, organizations must embrace asynchronous work and give employees more control over when and how they communicate.

Meeting-Free Days: Some companies have implemented meeting-free days to give employees uninterrupted time for focused work. These days are dedicated to deep work, allowing employees to complete tasks without the distraction of virtual meetings.

Quiet Hours: Quiet hours are specific blocks of time when no meetings are scheduled, and employees are encouraged to focus on their work. This approach helps employees' recharge mentally and create a sense of calm in an otherwise busy day.

Asynchronous Communication: Asynchronous communication tools like Slack, Loom, and project management platforms allow employees to collaborate without needing to be online at the same time. This reduces the need for constant video calls and lets employees respond to messages and updates on their own schedule.

Case Studies: Companies Reducing Digital Fatigue

- **Shopify**: Shopify has implemented "No Meeting Wednesdays," giving employees a break from meetings mid-week to focus on deep work. This initiative has helped reduce burnout and improve overall productivity.
- **GitLab**: GitLab is a fully remote company that encourages asynchronous communication and minimizes real-time meetings. Employees are trusted to manage their own schedules, reducing the need for constant digital engagement.

7 MANAGING DISTRIBUTED TEAMS ACROSS TIME ZONES

The Challenge of Time Zone Differences

As companies embrace remote work, many are hiring employees from different parts of the world. While this allows access to a global talent pool, it also presents a unique challenge: managing teams across multiple time zones.

When team members are spread across different regions, it can be difficult to schedule meetings, ensure alignment on projects, and maintain consistent communication. Employees in one time zone might be starting their day while others are finishing up. Without careful planning, this can lead to miscommunication, frustration, and a lack of cohesion within the team.

Best Practices for Managing Global Teams

Successfully managing distributed teams across time zones requires a shift in how work is structured and communicated. Here are some best practices for managing global teams:

Asynchronous Workflows: The key to managing distributed teams is embracing asynchronous work. This means creating workflows where employees can collaborate without needing to be online at the same time. Clear documentation, project management tools, and shared resources are essential for enabling asynchronous collaboration.

Overlap Hours: When possible, schedule overlap hours where all team members are online at the same time. This creates a window for real-time collaboration while allowing employees to work independently for the rest of the day. These hours should be carefully chosen to ensure that no team member is consistently working outside their regular time zone.

Clear Communication Channels: Establish clear communication protocols to avoid confusion. For example, use project management tools like Asana or Trello to keep everyone updated on the status of projects. Avoid relying solely on emails, which can quickly become overwhelming in a distributed team.

Challenges of Flexibility: Organizational Cohesion in Distributed Teams

As teams become more distributed across different locations and time zones, maintaining organizational cohesion becomes a significant challenge. The lack of face-to-face interaction can make it difficult to foster a sense of community, leading to feelings of isolation and disengagement, particularly for remote employees.

- **Asynchronous Communication**: Encouraging asynchronous communication can help bridge the time zone gap. Tools like project management software and shared digital workspaces allow team members to collaborate effectively even on different schedules. Clear guidelines for asynchronous communication ensure that important messages are not missed and that work progresses smoothly.

- **Building a Sense of Belonging**: HR must prioritize activities that foster connection and inclusion across distributed teams. Virtual team-building exercises, recognition programs, and regular one-on-one check-ins help build relationships and keep employees connected to the broader organizational mission.

HSBC: Navigating Flexibility in a Highly Regulated Industry

HSBC, one of the largest banking institutions in the world, adopted a hybrid work model in response to the pandemic. Recognizing the diverse needs of their global workforce, HSBC implemented "hot desks" for in-office work and invested heavily in remote working technologies. They also provided allowances to employees for setting up home offices, ensuring that workers had the necessary tools to remain productive.

In financial services, where regulatory concerns and data security are paramount, HSBC had to develop robust systems to protect sensitive information while allowing employees to work remotely. Their success in navigating these challenges demonstrates that even traditionally rigid industries can embrace flexibility without compromising on security.

Key Takeaway: Non-tech sectors, such as financial services, have faced significant regulatory and operational challenges in embracing remote work. Companies like HSBC are proving that with the right infrastructure and security protocols, even highly regulated industries can offer flexibility.

Case Studies: Companies Managing Distributed Teams

- **GitLab**: GitLab is a pioneer in managing distributed teams across time zones. The company operates asynchronously, with detailed documentation for every process, ensuring that employees can collaborate effectively, no matter where they are in the world.

- **InVision**: InVision is a fully distributed company with employees working in over 20 countries. The company uses Slack for real-time communication and Trello for project management, allowing team members to collaborate across time zones without friction.

8 THE HYBRID WORK MODEL – BALANCING REMOTE & IN-OFFICE WORK

The Rise of Hybrid Work

As companies navigate the post-pandemic world, many are choosing a hybrid work model, which blends remote and in-office work. Hybrid work offers the best of both worlds: the flexibility of remote work and the collaboration benefits of in-person meetings. However, creating a balance that works for both employees and employers is not always straightforward.

The hybrid model allows employees to decide when it's necessary to be physically present in the office, whether it's for meetings, brainstorming sessions, or team-building activities. On other days, they can work remotely, enjoying the benefits of flexibility and the opportunity to focus without office distractions.

Key Considerations for Hybrid Work Success

While hybrid work offers advantages, it also requires intentional planning and clear communication to avoid pitfalls like employee inequality, burnout, or misaligned expectations. Companies that embrace hybrid models need to address several key considerations:

- **Inclusion and Fairness**: One of the challenges of hybrid work is ensuring that both remote and in-office employees feel equally included. Remote workers may worry about being left out of impromptu office conversations or missing networking opportunities. HR teams need to create policies that ensure all employees—whether remote or in-office—are equally visible and have access to the same opportunities for recognition and advancement.

- **Communication and Collaboration**: Hybrid teams require robust communication channels that support both synchronous and asynchronous collaboration. Tools like Slack, Microsoft Teams, and Zoom play an important role in bridging the gap between remote and in-office workers. Clear guidelines should be established on when to meet in person and when virtual meetings suffice.

- **Office Space Redesign**: The traditional office setup doesn't work as well in a hybrid world. To support hybrid work, companies may need to rethink their office space. Instead of individual cubicles or permanent desks, offices might feature flexible workstations, hot desks, and collaboration zones where employees can work together when they're on-site.

- **Managing Performance and Expectations**: In a hybrid model, it's critical to set clear expectations around performance. Employees should know when they're expected to be in the office and what outcomes they need to deliver, regardless of location. Performance should be measured by results, not hours logged in a particular location.

Hybrid Work Models: Customizing the Approach

There is no one-size-fits-all approach to hybrid work. Companies must tailor their hybrid models to suit their specific business needs, workforce demographics, and operational goals. Some common hybrid work models include:

- **Office-First, Remote-Second**: Employees are expected to be in the office most of the time but can work remotely a few days a week. This model is suitable for companies that prioritize in-person collaboration but still want to offer some flexibility.

- **Remote-First, Office-Second**: In this model, remote work is the default, but employees are encouraged to come into the office for specific activities like team-building events or important meetings. This approach offers maximum flexibility while maintaining the benefits of occasional face-to-face interaction.

- **Fluid Hybrid**: This flexible model allows employees to choose when and where they work based on their personal preferences and project needs. Some employees may choose to work primarily from home, while others may prefer to be in the office more often.

Challenges of Flexibility: Fairness Between Remote and In-Office Employees

One of the biggest challenges in hybrid work models is ensuring fairness between remote and in-office employees. Remote workers may feel that they are missing out on opportunities for advancement, recognition, or spontaneous networking that can happen in the office. Similarly, in-office employees may feel that remote workers are getting a better deal by avoiding commutes and maintaining a more flexible schedule.

- **Equal Opportunities**: HR must ensure that performance evaluations and promotions are based on clear, objective criteria that do not favor in-office visibility. Regular feedback sessions, transparent promotion processes, and equal access to leadership opportunities are necessary to maintain fairness.

- **Preventing "Proximity Bias"**: Proximity bias—the tendency to favor those who are physically present—can be a major issue in hybrid work environments. HR can combat this by training managers to evaluate employees based on their contributions, not their location, and encouraging remote-friendly performance reviews.

By addressing these challenges, HR can ensure that hybrid work models foster an equitable and inclusive environment for all employees, regardless of where they work.

Siemens: Balancing Flexibility and On-Site Operations

Siemens, a global leader in manufacturing and technology, has embraced a hybrid work model, allowing employees in corporate roles to work remotely or in-office depending on their needs. Siemens implemented a policy called "New Normal," where employees are free to choose where they work for two or three days a week, depending on the nature of their role.

Despite being a manufacturing company, Siemens has embraced digital transformation, enabling flexible working conditions for office-based employees while maintaining strict on-site requirements for production staff. The key challenge for Siemens was ensuring that remote employees stayed engaged and connected with on-site workers. They tackled this by investing in advanced collaboration tools and fostering a culture that prioritizes both physical and digital spaces.

Key Takeaway: Even in industries where on-site work is critical (like manufacturing), hybrid models are possible. Companies like Siemens are showing how to balance in-person and remote work by allowing flexibility in non-production roles while keeping production lines running efficiently.

Case Studies: Companies Embracing Hybrid Work

- **Microsoft**: Microsoft has adopted a hybrid work model that allows employees to work from home up to 50% of the time. The company encourages teams to meet in person when necessary but also offers flexibility for remote work based on employee preferences and team needs.

- **HubSpot**: HubSpot offers a flexible hybrid work model, giving employees the option to work from home, come into the office, or do a mix of both. The company has redesigned its office spaces to create more collaboration zones and fewer individual workstations, emphasizing teamwork over presence.

9 THE ROLE OF HUMAN RESORUCES IN SUPPORTING FLEXIBILITY

Cultural Impacts: The Role of HR in Cultural Transformation

HR is the architect of organizational culture, making it a critical player in the shift toward flexible work. Moving from a rigid, office-based model to one that embraces flexibility requires HR to reframe company culture and practices to support a more fluid, adaptable environment.

- **Redefining Accountability**: In a flexible culture, accountability shifts from time-based metrics (e.g., hours logged) to result-based metrics (e.g., project completion and quality). HR must redefine performance evaluations and implement systems that reward outcomes, creativity, and problem-solving rather than hours worked.

- **Training Managers**: HR's role in training managers to lead flexible teams is essential. This training must focus on shifting managers from micromanagers to facilitators, teaching them to build trust, set clear expectations, and manage outcomes.

- **Promoting Inclusivity**: To foster an inclusive culture, HR must ensure that both remote and in-office employees have equal access to opportunities, feedback, and resources. Regular training on inclusive communication, remote onboarding, and equitable performance assessments helps ensure that flexible work is embraced by all employees, regardless of their location.

By prioritizing cultural change, HR can help organizations create environments where flexibility and employee autonomy thrive, fostering greater innovation, satisfaction, and loyalty.

HR as the Catalyst for Flexibility

HR professionals are uniquely positioned to lead the charge in creating flexible work environments. As the gatekeepers of company policies, employee well-being, and organizational culture, HR can shape the future of work by advocating for and implementing flexible work policies that benefit both employees and the business.

The shift to remote work has shown that flexibility is not just a trend but a permanent shift in how we approach work. HR must now focus on embedding flexibility into the company's DNA—moving beyond temporary adjustments to create long-lasting policies and practices that align with this new reality.

Crafting Flexible Work Policies

To truly embrace flexibility, HR must craft policies that accommodate a wide range of employee needs. These policies should account for remote work, hybrid models, and flexible schedules, while also ensuring equity and fairness.

- **Remote Work Policies**: HR should outline clear expectations for remote work, including guidelines on communication, performance metrics, and collaboration tools. This ensures that employees working from home have the structure they need while maintaining flexibility.

- **Hybrid Work Models**: For companies adopting a hybrid approach, HR can help create frameworks that balance in-office and remote work. This includes setting expectations for how often employees need to be in the office, as well as ensuring that those who work remotely are not disadvantaged in terms of career progression or visibility.

- **Flexible Hours**: Allowing employees to choose their working hours is another key element of flexibility. HR should develop policies that outline how flexible hours work, how to ensure team collaboration across different schedules, and how to track results instead of hours.

Training Managers to Lead with Trust and Autonomy

One of the biggest challenges in implementing flexible work policies is ensuring that managers are equipped to lead remote and hybrid teams. Traditionally, many managers equated productivity with physical presence. However, in a flexible work environment, managers must shift their focus from time-based metrics to outcome-based performance.

HR can play a pivotal role in training managers to lead with trust, autonomy, and empathy. This includes:

- **Trust-Based Management**: Encouraging managers to focus on the quality of work delivered rather than when or where it was done. This shift requires a mindset change, as many managers are accustomed to overseeing employees closely in an office setting.

- **Empathy and Well-Being**: HR can train managers to recognize the unique challenges that remote work can pose, including feelings of isolation, digital fatigue, or burnout. Empathy is key to creating a supportive work environment, and managers should be trained to check in on their teams' mental health as much as their productivity.

- **Clear Communication**: Effective communication is the backbone of remote work. HR can provide tools and templates to help managers communicate clearly and consistently with their teams, ensuring that everyone is aligned on goals and expectations.

Adam Grant, an organizational psychologist and leading voice on workplace culture, has been a vocal advocate for creating trust-based environments, especially in the context of flexible work. His research has consistently shown that trust and autonomy are key factors in driving employee engagement and performance. In a recent article, Grant highlighted the importance of building trust as the foundation for successful remote and flexible work.

"The best leaders don't control how their employees work; they create environments where people feel trusted to manage their own time and responsibilities. Flexibility is not just about where you work, but how you work. And when employees are trusted, they're more likely to be creative and motivated."

Grant's insights reinforce the idea that HR's role in flexible work environments isn't simply to manage logistics but to foster a culture of trust and autonomy that allows employees to thrive.

Flexible Performance Metrics

Performance management in a flexible work environment requires a shift away from tracking hours worked to measuring outcomes. HR can support this by developing flexible performance metrics that focus on the results employees deliver rather than how much time they spend on a task.

- **Outcome-Based KPIs**: Create performance metrics that are tied to specific goals, tasks, and deliverables. For example, instead of tracking how many hours an employee spends on a project, track the completion of key milestones or the quality of the final outcome.

- **Frequent Check-Ins**: HR should encourage managers to hold regular, informal check-ins with their teams rather than relying solely on annual performance reviews. This allows for real-time feedback and course correction, if necessary, while also supporting employees' growth and development in a more fluid work environment.

Case Studies: HR Champions of Flexibility

- **Microsoft**: As mentioned previously, Microsoft has implemented a flexible work policy that allows employees to work from home up to 50% of the time. HR played a key role in rolling out this policy by providing managers with tools for managing hybrid teams and tracking performance.

- **Dropbox**: Dropbox's "Virtual First" policy was driven by HR's recognition of the need for flexibility. HR developed comprehensive training for managers on how to lead distributed teams, and performance is measured based on results rather than hours worked.

10 REMOTE WORK & CAREER DEVELOPMENT

The "Out of Sight, Out of Mind" Problem

One of the challenges remote workers face is the fear of being overlooked for promotions or career development opportunities simply because they are not physically present in the office. The old adage "out of sight, out of mind" can be particularly true in organizations that have not fully adapted to remote work.

In an in-office environment, visibility often plays a significant role in promotions and recognition. Casual interactions with managers, hallway conversations, and spontaneous brainstorming sessions can all contribute to an employee's visibility and perceived value. But in a remote work setting, these opportunities for informal visibility are greatly reduced, which can lead to remote workers feeling isolated or undervalued.

Ensuring Remote Workers Are Not Left Behind

HR must ensure that remote employees are not disadvantaged when it comes to career development and promotions. This requires intentional efforts to create processes that are transparent, fair, and inclusive for all employees, regardless of where they work.

- **Equitable Access to Opportunities**: HR should implement policies that ensure remote workers have the same access to training, mentorship, and career advancement opportunities as their in-office counterparts. This could include virtual leadership development programs, online training courses, and remote-friendly mentorship opportunities.

- **Transparent Performance Reviews**: Performance reviews should be based on objective criteria and clearly communicated to all employees. HR can create standardized templates and evaluation forms that measure performance based on outcomes and contributions, rather than physical presence in the office.

- **Career Development Plans**: HR can encourage managers to work with their remote employees to create personalized career development plans. These plans should outline the employee's goals, the skills they need to develop, and the steps they can take to advance within the company. Regular check-ins between the employee and their manager can help ensure these plans stay on track.

John, a software engineer at a multinational company, was initially worried that working remotely would affect his visibility and chances for promotion. However, his company's focus on outcome-based performance reviews helped him grow in his career:

"At first, I thought working remotely would put me at a disadvantage, especially with fewer opportunities to network in person. But my manager was great at setting clear goals and outcomes. We had regular virtual check-ins, and I ended up getting promoted to a team lead because of the work I did—not because I was visible in the office."

John's experience shows that with the right management practices, remote workers can advance in their careers without being physically present in the office. His promotion underscores the value of outcome-based evaluations in creating equitable opportunities for remote employees.

Building a Remote-Friendly Leadership Pipeline

HR should focus on building a leadership pipeline that is inclusive of remote workers. This involves creating programs that prepare remote employees for leadership roles, ensuring they have the skills and visibility needed to advance in their careers.

- **Remote Leadership Development Programs**: HR can create leadership development programs specifically designed for remote workers. These programs should focus on the unique challenges of leading distributed teams, such as communication, collaboration, and building trust across distance.
- **Virtual Mentorship**: Mentorship is a key factor in career growth, but it can be more difficult to foster in a remote environment. HR can create virtual mentorship programs where remote employees

are paired with leaders in the company for regular one-on-one meetings. These mentorships provide valuable guidance and help remote workers build connections within the organization.

Southern New Hampshire University: Fostering Career Growth Remotely

NHU, one of the largest online universities in the U.S., was already operating primarily online before the pandemic. However, they have continually innovated to provide flexibility for both faculty and students. SNHU has built a remote-first faculty structure, where professors and staff can work from anywhere in the world. Career progression at SNHU is not tied to physical presence but rather to student success and outcome-based performance metrics.

SNHU offers virtual mentorship programs and leadership development tracks that are accessible to all employees, regardless of their location. This focus on outcome-driven career development has made it easier for remote staff to grow in their careers while staying fully connected to the organization's goals.

Key Takeaway: The education sector, particularly institutions offering online programs, has been a pioneer in remote work models. Institutions like SNHU show that by prioritizing outcome-based evaluations and offering remote-friendly professional development, career growth is achievable even in non-traditional work settings.

Case Studies: Career Development for Remote Workers

- **GitLab**: GitLab is a remote-first company that prioritizes career development for all employees. The company offers online training, virtual mentorship, and leadership development programs that are fully accessible to remote workers. Promotion criteria are transparent, and employees are evaluated based on their contributions rather than their location.
- **Zapier**: Zapier, another fully remote company, has implemented a mentorship program for remote employees that helps them develop leadership skills and navigate their career paths within

the company. Zapier's HR team ensures that remote workers have the same opportunities for growth as those working in the office.

11 NEW PERSPECTIVES – OLDER EMPLOYEES, GEN Z & THE RISE OF DIGITAL NOMADS

Remote Flexibility for Seasoned Professionals

Older employees, often those nearing retirement, can benefit significantly from remote and flexible work arrangements. These employees may have spent decades commuting to the office, and remote work offers them the ability to continue their careers while maintaining a better work-life balance. However, companies need to be mindful of the challenges older employees might face, particularly around technology.

- **Digital Literacy**: While older workers bring experience and institutional knowledge, they may struggle with new digital tools used in remote work. HR should provide adequate training and ongoing support to help older employees adapt to remote work technology.

- **Health and Flexibility**: Older employees often have health concerns or family caregiving responsibilities that make commuting difficult. Offering flexible work arrangements—such as part-time remote work or hybrid schedules—allows these employees to stay in the workforce longer while managing their personal responsibilities.

- **Knowledge Transfer**: Remote work can create barriers to the knowledge transfer between older employees and younger generations. HR can facilitate virtual mentorship programs where older employees share their expertise with younger colleagues through remote platforms.

Gen Z: The Digital-First Workforce

Gen Z, the newest generation entering the workforce, has grown up in a fully digital world. This generation is highly comfortable with technology, remote communication, and digital collaboration. For Gen Z workers, flexibility and work-life balance are not just perks—they are expectations.

- **Demand for Flexibility**: Gen Z workers are less likely to accept rigid, 9-to-5 office jobs. They prioritize jobs that offer flexibility, the ability to work from anywhere, and a focus on outcomes rather than hours. Companies that fail to offer flexible work models risk losing top Gen Z talent to competitors.

- **Digital Communication Skills**: Gen Z is adept at using digital communication tools, from Slack and Zoom to social media platforms. This generation values real-time feedback and frequent communication, which fits well with remote and hybrid work environments. HR should embrace these digital tools and create opportunities for more dynamic, ongoing conversations between managers and Gen Z employees.

- **Values-Driven Employment**: Gen Z workers are highly value-driven. They seek out companies that align with their personal values, whether that's a commitment to sustainability, diversity, or social impact. Employers must emphasize their company culture, mission, and values in the remote work environment to attract and retain Gen Z talent.

Sid Sijbrandij, CEO of GitLab, leads one of the largest all-remote companies in the world. He has long championed the idea that remote work is the great equalizer, allowing people from all corners of the globe to contribute equally regardless of their physical location. In interviews and public statements, Sijbrandij emphasizes how remote work opens up opportunities to access talent worldwide, removing geographic barriers and fostering diversity.

"Remote work is the great equalizer. It allows people from different backgrounds, countries, and time zones to contribute equally. By removing geographic barriers, we can tap into a global talent pool that was previously unreachable."

Sijbrandij's insight underscores the global reach and inclusivity of remote work, making it possible for companies to build diverse, distributed teams without the limitations of geography or physical office space.

The Rise of Digital Nomads

Digital nomadism is a growing trend, driven by the increased acceptance of remote work. Digital nomads are workers who take advantage of the ability to work from anywhere by traveling and living in different locations while maintaining their jobs. This lifestyle appeals to a wide range of workers, from young professionals to freelancers and entrepreneurs.

- **Legal and Tax Implications**: Digital nomads present unique challenges for employers, particularly when it comes to legal and tax compliance. HR must ensure that employees working from different countries or regions comply with local tax laws, visa requirements, and labor regulations. Offering clear guidelines on where employees can work remotely and for how long is essential to avoid complications.

- **Maintaining Engagement and Accountability**: While digital nomadism offers freedom, it also requires employees to remain accountable for their work despite their location. Employers must set clear expectations, deadlines, and communication protocols to ensure that digital nomads remain engaged and productive.

- **Creating a Supportive Environment**: To support digital nomads, companies should offer tools that allow for asynchronous work and flexible communication schedules. Digital nomads may work in different time zones, so offering flexibility around meeting times and deadlines is key to keeping them involved in the team's activities.

Case Studies: Companies Embracing Diverse Workforces

- **Dell**: Dell has implemented remote work policies that cater to a diverse workforce, including older employees and digital nomads. The company offers training and support to ensure that all employees, regardless of age or location, have the tools and resources they need to succeed.

- **Spotify:** Spotify's "Work From Anywhere" policy allows employees to choose where they work, including the option to live and work remotely for extended periods. This policy has been especially appealing to digital nomads and younger employee who value flexibility and the ability to travel while working.

12 TRUST VS SERVEILLANCE – THE BATTLE FOR REMOTE WORK AUTONOMY

The Rise of Employee Surveillance Tools

As remote work became more widespread, some companies turned to surveillance tools to monitor their employees' productivity. These tools can track everything from keystrokes to screen time, webcam usage, and even the number of emails sent in a day. The justification behind this monitoring is often a fear that employees will slack off or be less productive when working from home.

However, employee surveillance has significant downsides. It erodes trust between employees and management, creates a culture of fear and anxiety, and can lead to burnout. Constant monitoring sends the message that employees are not trusted to manage their own time, which undermines their autonomy and motivation.

The Case for Trust-Based Management

In a results-oriented, flexible work environment, trust is key. Employees should be trusted to complete their tasks and manage their workloads without being constantly monitored. When employees feel trusted, they are more likely to be engaged, motivated, and productive.

- **Focus on Results, Not Activity**: Instead of tracking every minute an employee spends at their computer, companies should focus on the outcomes employees deliver. By setting clear goals and expectations, managers can measure performance based on what employees achieve, not how many hours they spend online.

- **Empowering Employees with Autonomy**: Autonomy is a major driver of employee engagement. When employees are given the freedom to decide how and when they work, they are more likely to take ownership of their tasks and feel a sense of responsibility for their results. This leads to higher job satisfaction and better performance.

Alternatives to Surveillance

Rather than resorting to invasive surveillance tools, companies should adopt strategies that foster trust and accountability while respecting employees' autonomy.

- **Regular Check-Ins**: Instead of monitoring employees' every move, managers can hold regular check-ins to discuss progress, provide feedback, and address any challenges. These check-ins allow for open communication and help managers stay informed without the need for constant surveillance.

- **Outcome-Based Performance Metrics**: As mentioned earlier, HR should develop performance metrics that are tied to outcomes, not time spent working. This shift ensures that employees are judged based on the quality and timeliness of their work, rather than how many hours they log in front of a screen.

Case Studies: Trust-Based Cultures

- **Basecamp**: Basecamp has long been an advocate for trust-based management. The company gives employees complete autonomy over their schedules and focuses on results rather than hours worked. Basecamp has rejected surveillance tools, believing that trust leads to better performance and happier employees.

- **Buffer**: Buffer is another company that operates on trust. Employees have the flexibility to work when and where they want, and the company has no interest in monitoring their activity. Instead, Buffer focuses on the outcomes employees deliver and maintains a culture of transparency and openness.

13 LEGAL & COMPLIANCE CHALLENGES IN REMOTE WORK

The Legal Landscape of Remote Work

As more companies embrace remote work, HR must navigate a complex legal landscape that includes labor laws, tax regulations, and data security requirements. When employees are working across different states, provinces, or even countries, ensuring compliance with local laws becomes a critical responsibility for HR.

Tax Implications of Remote Work

One of the most significant legal challenges in remote work is determining the tax obligations for employees working in different jurisdictions. In some cases, employees who work in a different province, state or country than their employer may be subject to different tax laws, and employers may need to withhold taxes accordingly.

- **State and Local Taxes**: HR must be aware of the tax laws in each state or country where employees are working. This includes understanding the requirements for income tax withholding, unemployment insurance, and other state-specific obligations.

- **Permanent Establishment Risk**: For companies with employees working in foreign countries, there is a risk of creating a "permanent establishment" in that country. This could trigger corporate tax liabilities and other legal obligations. HR should work closely with legal and tax professionals to understand the implications of employees working abroad.

Labor Laws and Employee Classification

Remote work also raises questions about labor laws and employee classification. Different jurisdictions have different rules regarding employee rights, working hours, and overtime pay. HR must ensure that remote employees are classified correctly and that their rights are protected, regardless of where they are working.

- **Employee vs. Independent Contractor**: In some cases, companies may classify remote workers as independent contractors rather than employees. However, misclassification can lead to legal consequences, including fines and back pay. HR should ensure that workers are classified correctly based on the laws of the jurisdiction in which they are working.

- **Overtime and Wage Laws**: HR must also ensure compliance with local labor laws regarding overtime and wages. This is especially important for non-exempt employees, who may be entitled to overtime pay if they work beyond a certain number of hours per day or week.

Data Security and Privacy Concerns

Remote work introduces new challenges when it comes to data security and privacy. Companies must ensure that employees working from home are following the same data protection protocols as those in the office.

- **Secure Networks and Devices**: HR should work with IT departments to ensure that remote workers have secure access to company systems. This includes providing VPNs, encrypting sensitive data, and ensuring that employees use company-issued devices for work-related tasks.

- **Compliance with Data Protection Laws**: For companies operating internationally, HR must ensure compliance with data protection laws such as the General Data Protection Regulation (GDPR) in Europe or the California Consumer Privacy Act (CCPA) in the United States. Remote workers must handle personal data in compliance with these regulations, regardless of where they are working.

Future Trends: Speculation on the Future Legal Landscape of Work

As the world of work evolves, so too will the legal frameworks that govern it. The rise of remote work, digital nomadism, and global talent pools will require governments to rethink tax structures, labor laws, and data privacy regulations.

- **Global Tax Reforms**: The growing number of employees working remotely across borders will likely push governments to reform tax laws. This could include new regulations on cross-border income, residency-based taxation, and employer obligations for remote workers living in different countries. HR teams will need to stay ahead of these changes to ensure compliance.

- **Data Privacy Regulations**: As remote work increases the use of digital tools, stricter data privacy regulations will emerge to protect employees and organizations. HR must work closely with legal and IT teams to ensure that sensitive employee data is protected and that the company complies with data privacy laws like GDPR or the California Consumer Privacy Act.

- **Labor Law Adaptations**: Flexible work will also lead to changes in labor laws, particularly around employee classification, overtime regulations, and work-from-home stipends. HR teams will need to anticipate these changes and adapt company policies to remain compliant while providing the flexibility that employees demand.

Case Studies: Navigating Legal Challenges

- **Shopify**: Shopify has a globally distributed workforce, and HR plays a key role in ensuring compliance with local labor laws and tax regulations. The company works closely with legal experts to navigate the complexities of remote work across different jurisdictions.

- **Salesforce**: Salesforce's HR team ensures that remote employees are classified correctly and follow the appropriate labor laws, including those related to overtime and wages. The company has also implemented robust data security protocols to protect sensitive information for remote workers.

14 THE FUTURE OF OFFICE SPACES – FROM DESKS TO COLLABORATION HUBS

Rethinking the Role of the Office

The pandemic has fundamentally changed the way we view office spaces. No longer seen as the primary place where work happens, offices are being reimagined as hubs for collaboration, creativity, and socialization. In this new model, employees may no longer need to be in the office every day but can use the office as a space to connect with colleagues, engage in collaborative projects, and attend meetings that benefit from face-to-face interaction.

This shift represents a significant departure from the traditional model of the office as a place to clock in and work independently for eight hours. Instead, the office becomes a dynamic space that complements remote work, rather than competing with it.

The Rise of the Hybrid Office

Hybrid work models, which combine remote work with periodic in-office attendance, are becoming more common as companies recognize the benefits of both remote and in-person work. In a hybrid model, employees may come into the office a few days a week, or only for specific meetings or events. This allows for flexibility while still maintaining the option for face-to-face collaboration when needed.

Hybrid offices are designed to support these occasional visits, with more emphasis on communal areas and meeting rooms rather than individual desks. Employees are no longer tied to a single workstation; instead, they have access to flexible workspaces, such as open areas, conference rooms, and hot desks.

Designing Offices for Flexibility and Collaboration

To accommodate the needs of a hybrid workforce, office spaces need to be designed with flexibility in mind. This includes creating environments that foster collaboration, creativity, and innovation.

- **Flexible Meeting Spaces**: Offices can be redesigned to include a variety of meeting spaces, from small huddle rooms to large conference rooms equipped with video conferencing technology. These spaces should be adaptable, allowing for different configurations based on the size and needs of the group.

- **Hot Desks and Shared Workspaces**: Instead of assigning individual desks to employees, many offices are moving toward hot desking, where employees can choose a workstation when they come into the office. This allows for more efficient use of space and gives employees the freedom to work in different areas based on their needs.

- **Social Spaces**: Offices should also include areas where employees can socialize and build relationships. These spaces may include lounges, kitchens, or informal seating areas where employees can gather for casual conversations or impromptu brainstorming sessions.

Jason Fried, co-founder of Basecamp and author of Remote: Office Not Required, has long been a critic of traditional office setups. Fried argues that the office of the future should be designed with collaboration, not routine desk work, in mind. As one of the pioneers of remote work, his vision offers a refreshing alternative to the typical 9-to-5 office structure. In an interview about the changing nature of workspaces, Fried shared his thoughts on how offices should evolve in a post-remote world:

"The office should no longer be a place where people come to sit in front of computers all day—that's outdated. The office of the future is where people come to connect, brainstorm, and create together. It's a place for collaboration, not just work."

Fried's perspective aligns with the growing trend of transforming offices into spaces optimized for creativity, collaboration, and human connection, supporting the hybrid work model where physical presence is no longer the default expectation.

Kaiser Permanente: Reimagining Office Spaces for Healthcare Workers

Kaiser Permanente, a major healthcare provider, has embraced a hybrid work model for their administrative and office staff. Although healthcare delivery requires in-person presence, Kaiser Permanente realized that many administrative roles could be done remotely. They reimagined their office spaces to be used as collaboration hubs, where employees come in for meetings, brainstorming sessions, and training, but do most of their work remotely.

Kaiser Permanente has also invested in telemedicine technologies, allowing healthcare providers to deliver care remotely where possible. This shift has not only improved work flexibility for healthcare workers but has also enhanced patient care by expanding access to telehealth services.

Key Takeaway: The healthcare industry, typically known for requiring in-person work, is also adapting to flexible models where possible. By redesigning office spaces and leveraging telemedicine, healthcare organizations like Kaiser Permanente are balancing remote work with patient care.

Future Trends: Speculation on the Evolving Workforce and Technology

As we look to the future of work, it's clear that flexibility will remain a driving force in how companies structure their operations and manage talent. However, this future will also be shaped by advancements in technology, shifting workforce demographics, and evolving societal expectations.

- **Artificial Intelligence and Automation**: AI will continue to revolutionize the workplace by automating routine tasks, enabling smarter project management, and even enhancing communication. However, this could also lead to the displacement of certain jobs. HR must prepare to upskill workers and adapt job roles to complement AI-driven processes while maintaining human-centered roles in areas like creativity, leadership, and emotional intelligence.

- **The Rise of Gig and Project-Based Work**: With technology enabling more flexible work arrangements, we may see a rise in gig-based or project-based work structures where employees move between different projects, teams, or even companies. This shift will require companies to rethink their approach to talent management, employee benefits, and career development.

- **Changing Workforce Expectations**: Gen Z and future generations will expect more flexibility, autonomy, and purpose-driven work. HR leaders will need to create environments where these expectations are met, ensuring that future work models continue to prioritize employee well-being, diversity, and inclusivity.

By embracing these trends and preparing for future challenges, organizations can build a more adaptive, inclusive, and forward-thinking workplace that thrives in the age of flexibility.

Case Studies: Reimagining Office Spaces

- **Dropbox**: Dropbox has fully embraced the hybrid model with its "Virtual First" policy. Employees are encouraged to work remotely, but the company's offices, now called Dropbox Studios, have been redesigned as collaborative hubs. These studios are used for team gatherings, meetings, and social events, rather than everyday work.

- **Google**: Google has long been known for its innovative office spaces, and the company is now focusing on creating more flexible, hybrid-friendly environments. Google is redesigning its offices to include more outdoor spaces, collaborative areas, and meeting rooms equipped with state-of-the-art video conferencing technology.

15 REMOTE WORK AND ENVIRONMENTAL SUSTAINABILITY

The Environmental Benefits of Remote Work

Remote work has not only changed how we work but also how we impact the environment. During the pandemic, the shift to remote work led to a significant reduction in carbon emissions, as fewer people commuted to work, and companies scaled back their use of office buildings. This reduction in daily commuting, office energy use, and resource consumption has made remote work a key factor in corporate sustainability efforts.

For companies committed to reducing their carbon footprint, remote work offers a powerful solution. By allowing employees to work from home or choose flexible schedules, businesses can reduce the environmental impact of commuting, decrease office space requirements, and lower energy consumption.

Reducing Commuting and Traffic Congestion

One of the most obvious environmental benefits of remote work is the reduction in commuting. Fewer people on the roads means less traffic congestion, lower fuel consumption, and fewer greenhouse gas emissions. In major cities, the reduction in daily commutes during the pandemic led to cleaner air and fewer traffic-related accidents.

For employees, the shift to remote work also means saving money on fuel, parking, and public transportation. It's a win-win situation: employees gain time and financial savings, while the environment benefits from reduced emissions.

The Impact of Office Buildings

Office buildings are significant consumers of energy, water, and other resources. Heating, cooling, lighting, and powering office equipment require vast amounts of energy, much of which comes from nonrenewable sources. By downsizing office spaces or adopting hybrid work models, companies can reduce their environmental footprint and move toward more sustainable operations.

Many companies are now reevaluating the need for large, energy-intensive office spaces. By reducing the number of employees who work in the office daily, companies can cut back on energy consumption and reduce their reliance on large commercial real estate.

Potential Downsides: The Carbon Footprint of Digital Infrastructure

While remote work offers many environmental benefits, it's important to recognize that it also comes with its own environmental costs. The increased use of digital tools and cloud computing has led to a rise in energy consumption in data centers and other IT infrastructure. Video conferencing, file sharing, and online collaboration platforms require vast amounts of energy to operate, contributing to the carbon footprint of remote work.

To mitigate these effects, companies can adopt energy-efficient technologies and work with cloud service providers that prioritize sustainability. Encouraging employees to use energy-efficient devices and reduce unnecessary digital activity can also help minimize the environmental impact of remote work.

Case Studies: Companies Using Remote Work to Promote Sustainability

- **Salesforce**: Salesforce has committed to achieving 100% renewable energy across its operations, and its shift to a more flexible work model is part of its broader sustainability strategy. By reducing office space and promoting remote work, Salesforce is helping to lower its carbon footprint.
- **Dell**: Dell has integrated sustainability into its remote work strategy, reducing its office space and encouraging employees to work from home. The company is also focused on using energy-efficient technologies and partnering with cloud providers that prioritize environmental responsibility.

16 BUILDING A STRONG EMPLOYEE EXPERIENCE IN REMOTE TEAMS

The Importance of Employee Experience in Remote Work

Employee experience (EX) is a critical factor in the success of any organization. In a remote-first or hybrid work environment, creating a positive employee experience is even more important, as employees no longer have the daily, in-person interactions that help foster a sense of belonging and connection. HR leaders and managers must be intentional in their efforts to maintain a strong EX for remote teams.

A strong employee experience helps build engagement, loyalty, and productivity, while also reducing turnover and burnout. In a remote work setting, EX encompasses everything from onboarding and communication to recognition and career development.

Virtual Onboarding for Remote Employees

Onboarding is one of the most critical moments in an employee's journey, and it's even more important for remote employees who may never set foot in the office. HR teams must ensure that virtual onboarding processes are comprehensive, engaging, and supportive, helping new hires feel welcomed and connected to the company.

- **Welcome Kits**: Many companies are sending out physical welcome kits to new remote employees, which can include company swag, essential tech equipment, and personalized notes from their team. This helps create a sense of excitement and belonging right from the start.

- **Virtual Orientation Programs**: HR can create virtual orientation programs that introduce new hires to the company's culture, values, and mission. These programs can include interactive sessions with leaders, team-building activities, and training on the tools and systems they'll need to succeed.

Fostering Connection and Collaboration in Remote Teams

One of the biggest challenges in remote work is maintaining strong connections between employees. Without the daily face-to-face interactions of an office, remote workers can feel isolated or disconnected from their colleagues. HR and managers must take proactive steps to foster collaboration and build relationships within remote teams.

- **Regular Check-Ins**: Managers should hold regular one-on-one check-ins with their team members to discuss progress, provide feedback, and offer support. These check-ins help employees feel valued and stay connected to their team.

- **Virtual Team-Building Activities**: HR can organize virtual team-building activities to help remote employees bond and collaborate. These activities can include virtual happy hours, online games, or workshops that encourage creativity and teamwork.

- **Peer Recognition Programs**: Recognition is a powerful motivator, and HR can implement peer recognition programs that allow employees to celebrate each other's achievements. These programs can be virtual, with employees giving shout-outs on internal communication platforms or during team meetings.

Maria, a marketing strategist for a global brand, has thrived in her remote work environment, thanks to her company's focus on maintaining a strong employee experience. She shares:

"We have virtual happy hours, team-building exercises, and regular one-on-one check-ins with managers. The company culture has remained strong even though we're all remote. I've never felt disconnected, and in some ways, I feel more engaged now than when we were all in the office."

Maria's story demonstrates how intentional efforts to build community and maintain regular communication can keep employees engaged and connected, even in remote work settings. Her experience highlights the importance of fostering an inclusive, supportive culture for remote teams.

Case Studies: Creating a Positive Employee Experience for Remote Teams

- **InVision**: InVision, a fully remote company, has built a strong employee experience by focusing on virtual onboarding, regular team-building activities, and an open, transparent communication culture. The company also offers flexible work hours and encourages employees to take time for self-care and mental health.

- **HubSpot**: HubSpot has created a robust remote employee experience by offering virtual onboarding, career development programs, and an employee-driven recognition platform. The company also provides wellness stipends and access to mental health resources for all remote employees.

17 BUILDING A STRONG EMPLOYEE EXPERIENCE IN REMOTE TEAMS

As the future of work becomes increasingly flexible, with remote and hybrid models gaining traction, front-line workers find themselves in a vastly different position from their office-based counterparts. While knowledge workers have been quick to embrace remote work, front-line workers—those whose roles require a physical presence—are bound to the worksite. This divide raises important questions about fairness, employee perception, and how companies can address the needs of both groups.

The Dichotomy Between Front-Line and Knowledge Workers

The future of work looks promising for those in knowledge-based roles, where tasks can be completed from virtually anywhere, often with increased autonomy and flexibility. Front-line workers, on the other hand, continue to perform essential, in-person services, such as healthcare, retail, logistics, and manufacturing. This divide has become more pronounced in the post-pandemic world, as companies increasingly adopt hybrid or fully remote models for knowledge workers.

Key Roles Defined:

- **Front-line workers** are those who engage directly with customers, patients, or physical products. They perform critical tasks that require in-person work, such as nurses, warehouse workers, grocery store employees, and factory staff.
- **Knowledge workers** include professionals whose work primarily involves handling or processing information, such as software engineers, marketers, financial analysts, and researchers.

Why Can't Front-Line Workers Work Remotely?

The inherent nature of front-line work means that many tasks can't be done remotely. Interactions with customers, handling physical goods, and providing direct services often require workers to be present on-site.

However, while the operational needs of front-line workers demand physical presence, this has led to perceived inequality in how different worker types are treated. Remote and hybrid models are often seen as a perk, allowing knowledge workers to benefit from flexible schedules and improved work-life balance, while front-line workers must adhere to fixed schedules.

Balancing Fairness and Practicality:

- **Operational necessity**: For example, healthcare workers, factory staff, and logistics personnel can't perform their jobs remotely. The essential nature of their tasks requires physical presence, making remote work impractical.

- **Perception of inequality**: Front-line workers often feel left out of discussions about flexible work. While knowledge workers enjoy the advantages of remote work, front-line employees may feel they are shouldering more risk or responsibility by being physically present at work.

The Perception of Fairness Among Front-Line Workers

For front-line workers, seeing colleagues in office-based roles enjoy the flexibility of working remotely can lead to frustration. Many front-line workers feel that their contributions are undervalued in comparison to knowledge workers. The sense of inequality can affect morale, leading to disengagement and increased turnover.

Common Concerns Among Front-Line Workers:

- **Workplace safety and risks**: Especially during crises like the COVID-19 pandemic, front-line workers often face health risks that office workers do not. This disparity has heightened perceptions of unfair treatment.

- **Lack of flexibility**: Front-line workers often have less control over their schedules. Fixed shifts, long hours, and limited time off are common, while knowledge workers may have the ability to work from home or set their own hours.

- **Feeling less valued**: Front-line workers may perceive that their roles are seen as less important compared to the contributions of knowledge workers, even though they provide essential services.

Example: During the pandemic, many grocery store workers and healthcare staff expressed frustration at being labeled "essential" but not receiving equivalent compensation or flexibility compared to knowledge workers who could stay safely at home.

Addressing the Divide: Creating Fairness for Front-Line Workers

To foster a sense of equity, companies need to consider how to support front-line workers in ways that address their specific needs and challenges. While front-line workers may not be able to benefit from remote work, companies can offer compensation, benefits, and flexibility in other forms.

Strategies for Creating Fairness:

- **Enhanced compensation**: Offering higher wages, hazard pay (in situations like the pandemic), or bonuses for front-line workers can help balance the disparity between office and front-line workers.

- **Increased scheduling flexibility**: Allowing flexible or compressed shifts, implementing more control over schedules, and offering additional paid leave can help front-line workers feel that their needs are being met.

- **Well-being initiatives**: Front-line workers face higher physical and mental demands. Offering well-being programs, including mental health support, wellness stipends, or physical health initiatives, can show appreciation and support.

- **Recognition programs**: Regularly recognizing and celebrating the contributions of front-line workers through awards, spot bonuses, or public acknowledgment can help build morale and make them feel more valued.

Case Example: Walmart, one of the world's largest employers, employs both front-line and knowledge workers. To support front-line staff during the pandemic, Walmart introduced higher wages, bonuses, and increased paid sick leave. Additionally, they implemented wellness programs aimed at improving the mental and physical health of their front-line employees. This approach helped balance the disparity between the benefits knowledge workers were receiving and the in-person demands on front-line staff.

Companies Employing Both Front-Line and Knowledge Workers

For companies that manage both front-line and knowledge workers, balancing the needs of these two distinct groups is a complex challenge. Below are examples of companies that have successfully navigated these challenges:

Amazon's workforce is split between corporate office workers and warehouse/front-line employees. During the pandemic, Amazon implemented wage increases and bonuses for warehouse workers while also expanding their healthcare benefits. However, the company has faced scrutiny over working conditions for front-line staff, highlighting the challenges in creating true fairness between the two groups.

In the healthcare sector, organizations like Kaiser Permanente have explored ways to give flexibility to administrative and knowledge workers (e.g., allowing telemedicine for non-front-line roles) while maintaining in-person care for front-line healthcare workers. This model balances the need for essential services with the flexibility of remote work for support staff.

The Role of Technology in Supporting Front-Line Workers

Tech-Driven Flexibility for Front-Line Roles While remote work is not an option for most front-line roles, technology can provide alternative forms of flexibility. Automation, robotics, and AI are slowly being introduced into sectors like manufacturing and logistics to reduce the physical demands on workers and allow more time for strategic or managerial tasks that can potentially be done remotely.

The Future of Automation in Front-Line Roles In some industries, automation and robotics may reduce the need for constant in-person presence. For example, warehouses using robotic systems may allow some staff to manage operations remotely, while AI in healthcare can assist with diagnostics, giving front-line workers more flexible job roles in the future.

The Path Forward: Building an Inclusive Future for All Workers

As companies continue to shape the future of work, they must consider the diverse needs of their workforce. While remote work is a huge advancement for knowledge workers, front-line workers require different forms of support to ensure equity and fairness in the workplace.

Long-Term Considerations:

- How can companies continue to innovate in ways that support front-line workers with enhanced benefits, compensation, and flexibility?

- Will emerging technologies create new opportunities for front-line roles to incorporate remote or flexible elements?

- How can companies ensure that front-line workers feel valued and recognized for their contributions, even if they can't work remotely?

18 RETHINKING OFFICE SPACE IN A REMOTE FIRST WORLD

The Office Real Estate Dilemma

As remote work becomes the norm, companies are facing difficult decisions about their investments in large office spaces, particularly in urban centers. Many businesses have invested heavily in office towers, real estate, and infrastructure designed for a workforce that is no longer tethered to a physical location. Meanwhile, governments are concerned about the economic impact on urban districts that once thrived on the presence of office workers—restaurants, retailers, and services that depend on the daily influx of commuters.

Key Concerns:

- **Corporate Investment**: Companies worry about the financial implications of underutilized office space, especially in cities where prime real estate comes with a hefty price tag.
- **Economic Impact on Districts**: The shift away from in-office work affects entire neighborhoods that rely on the daily activity of office workers, potentially leading to decreased revenue for local businesses and a decline in urban vibrancy.

Creative Ideas for Repurposing Office Buildings

To avoid the stagnation of unused office spaces, there are numerous creative, adaptive solutions that can benefit both businesses and communities.

a) **Co-Working and Flexible Office Spaces**

- Repurpose Offices for Flexibility: Instead of abandoning office buildings, companies can redesign them into flexible, co-working spaces where employees or freelancers can come in when needed. These spaces can be rented out to startups, independent workers, and smaller companies that don't require full-time office space but need a professional environment occasionally.

b) **Mixed-Use Development**

- Converting Office Buildings into Mixed-Use Spaces: Office buildings can be transformed into multi-functional hubs that include residential apartments, retail spaces, and entertainment venues. This could breathe new life into business districts by bringing in permanent residents and increasing foot traffic at all hours of the day, not just during work hours.

c) **Green Spaces and Public Use**

- Urban Gardens and Community Spaces: One of the most innovative solutions is converting office rooftops or lobbies into urban gardens, green spaces, or public venues for events. These spaces can be repurposed to support environmental sustainability initiatives, providing city dwellers with green areas that enhance urban well-being.

d) **Housing Solutions**

- Transforming Office Buildings into Residential Housing: The growing demand for housing, particularly affordable housing, presents a unique opportunity. Empty office spaces can be converted into residential units, helping to alleviate housing shortages in urban areas. Governments and developers can work together to rezone commercial buildings for residential use, addressing both the housing crisis and the issue of vacant office space.

e) **Cultural and Educational Hubs**

- Art Galleries, Maker Spaces, and Education Centers: Some office buildings could be reimagined as cultural spaces, housing art galleries, maker labs, or community education centers. These venues could help foster creativity, innovation, and learning within the heart of cities while supporting the local economy with activities beyond traditional commerce.

Repurposing for the Greater Good: Altruism and Social Responsibility

As companies and governments rethink the use of office buildings in a world increasingly dominated by remote work, there's an opportunity not just to repurpose these spaces for profit but to contribute to society in meaningful ways. Altruism and a sense of social responsibility can drive innovative solutions that benefit vulnerable populations and communities in need.

Repurposing for Community and Social Services

Many office buildings can be transformed into spaces that provide critical services to those in need, particularly in urban centers where homelessness, lack of affordable housing, and access to essential resources are significant challenges.

- **Shelters and Affordable Housing**: Large office spaces, particularly those located in central urban areas, can be converted into shelters or affordable housing units. This can address the growing need for housing in many cities and provide a safe haven for vulnerable populations, including homeless individuals, low-income families, and refugees.

- **Community Resource Centers**: Former office buildings could also be turned into multi-purpose community centers, offering services such as job training, legal aid, food distribution, and healthcare. These centers can serve as vital support hubs for people in need, ensuring that essential services are accessible to all.

Charity and Social Enterprises

Office spaces can be leased or donated to charities, nonprofits, or social enterprises that are focused on solving societal challenges. By offering these organizations affordable or even free space, companies can contribute directly to positive social outcomes.

- **Charitable Hubs**: Businesses could collaborate with nonprofits to create charitable hubs within their unused spaces, fostering a culture of giving back while supporting organizations that tackle hunger, poverty, education, and health.

- **Social Enterprise Incubators**: Office buildings could also house incubators for social enterprises—businesses with a mission to solve societal problems. These spaces could be used to cultivate startups focused on sustainable development, healthcare access, clean energy, or educational equality.

Creating Inclusive, Supportive Spaces for Vulnerable Populations

In addition to physical space, there is a growing recognition that societal well-being extends beyond just housing and charity—it's about creating inclusive environments that help people thrive.

- **Support for Marginalized Communities**: Repurposed office spaces could be used to provide safe, supportive environments for marginalized groups such as LGBTQ+ youth, individuals recovering from addiction, or survivors of domestic violence. These spaces could offer not only housing but also counseling, mentorship, and educational opportunities.

- **Mental Health and Wellness Centers**: With the rise in mental health concerns, office buildings could be reimagined as wellness centers focused on providing mental health services to those who cannot afford them. Offering accessible therapy, mental health education, and peer support networks would be a direct way to give back to the community.

Environmental and Societal Sustainability

Repurposing office buildings for social good not only helps vulnerable populations but also contributes to broader sustainability goals, benefiting society as a whole.

- **Reducing Urban Waste**: By reusing and repurposing existing buildings rather than constructing new ones, cities can reduce the environmental impact associated with construction. This promotes a circular economy where existing resources are maximized for greater societal benefit.

- **Green Energy and Community Gardens**: Office spaces could incorporate green energy solutions, like solar panels, or create urban rooftop gardens that provide fresh produce to food banks or local communities. This not only addresses food insecurity but also contributes to environmental sustainability.

Collaborative Partnerships Between Businesses and Governments

One of the most powerful ways to repurpose office spaces for societal benefit is through partnerships between the private sector, governments, and non-profit organizations.

- **Public-Private Partnerships**: Governments can incentivize businesses to repurpose office spaces for charitable uses through tax benefits, grants, or low-interest loans. This collaboration can amplify the impact, creating more sustainable urban developments focused on the well-being of vulnerable populations.
- **Corporate Social Responsibility**: For companies, transforming office spaces into community centers or shelters could become a key part of their **corporate social responsibility (CSR)** strategy. Businesses that invest in their local communities by supporting charitable endeavors can strengthen their brand while making a tangible impact on societal well-being.

Supporting Local Economies in a Remote World

Governments and local authorities are also tasked with rethinking how they manage city planning in a world where fewer workers are commuting daily. To adapt, they can invest in initiatives that encourage diverse use of commercial districts, ensuring economic vibrancy.

Incentives for Mixed-Use Development

- Government Grants and Tax Incentives: To encourage companies and real estate developers to convert office spaces, governments could offer tax incentives or grants for creating mixed-use spaces or affordable housing in these areas. This would help to balance the economic needs of urban districts and support the diversification of city spaces.

A Win-Win for Cities and Companies

Ultimately, the repurposing of office buildings presents an opportunity for both cities and companies to innovate and create more sustainable, vibrant urban environments. By transitioning away from the rigid, centralized office model, cities can evolve into more flexible, mixed-use spaces that cater to a broader range of needs—from work to community life, housing, and leisure.

While the transition to remote and hybrid work may seem like a threat to the traditional office, it's also a unique opportunity to reimagine what urban spaces can become. By repurposing office buildings into multi-functional, community-driven hubs, companies and governments can create a more adaptive, resilient, and compassionate future for cities. This transformation helps businesses maximize their real estate investments while ensuring urban centers remain vibrant, economically viable, and socially responsible in a post-office world.

Beyond practical solutions, the reimagining of office spaces also presents a chance to support vulnerable populations, address societal challenges, and foster altruism. By transforming these spaces into community resource centers, housing for those in need, or charitable hubs, we can extend the flexibility that remote work has brought to individuals and use it to empower entire communities.

As companies and cities navigate this transformation, the opportunity to repurpose office spaces is more than just a financial or logistical solution— it's a pathway to creating more inclusive, supportive, and sustainable urban environments, redefining how we work and how we care for each other.

19 RESILENCE AND ADAPTABILITY – KEY COMPETENCIES FOR REMOTE WORK

The Importance of Resilience in Remote Work

Remote work requires a different set of skills than traditional office work. One of the most critical competencies for remote workers is resilience—the ability to adapt to changing circumstances, stay focused in the face of challenges, and bounce back from setbacks. Resilience is essential for navigating the complexities of remote work, including managing time, staying productive, and maintaining work-life balance.

In a remote environment, employees must be self-motivated, resourceful, and able to work independently without the immediate support of colleagues or managers. Resilience helps employees stay engaged and positive, even when faced with obstacles.

Building Resilience in Remote Teams

HR can play a key role in fostering resilience among remote employees by providing training, resources, and support.

- **Resilience Training**: HR can offer training programs that help employees develop resilience and adaptability. These programs can include techniques for managing stress, staying focused, and maintaining a positive mindset during challenging times.

- **Encouraging Self-Care**: HR can promote self-care practices that support resilience, such as encouraging employees to take regular breaks, practice mindfulness, and set boundaries between work and personal life. Providing access to mental health resources and wellness programs can also help employees build resilience.

Adaptability: Thriving in a Changing Work Environment

Adaptability is another key competency for remote work. The ability to adjust to new tools, workflows, and processes is essential for thriving in a remote-first environment. As companies continue to evolve, employees who can adapt to change will be more successful and more likely to advance in their careers.

HR can help employees build adaptability by offering continuous learning opportunities, fostering a growth mindset, and encouraging experimentation and innovation.

- **Continuous Learning**: HR should provide access to online training and development programs that allow employees to build new skills and stay up-to-date with industry trends. This helps employees remain adaptable and prepared for future changes.

- **Promoting a Growth Mindset**: A growth mindset—the belief that abilities can be developed through effort and learning—is critical for adaptability. HR can promote this mindset by recognizing employees for their efforts, encouraging them to take on new challenges, and providing opportunities for growth and development.

Case Studies: Building Resilience and Adaptability in Remote Teams

- **Buffer**: Buffer has a strong focus on building resilience and adaptability within its remote team. The company offers resilience training, promotes a culture of self-care, and encourages employees to take time off when needed. Buffer also fosters adaptability by providing access to continuous learning and encouraging employees to experiment with new tools and workflows.

- **Trello**: Trello, part of Atlassian, emphasizes adaptability in its remote team. The company encourages employees to stay curious, learn new skills, and embrace change. Trello also offers mental health support and flexible work hours to help employees maintain resilience and balance.

CONCLUSION: A CALL TO ACTION FOR A MORE HUMAN-FOCUSED WORKPLACE

The future of work is flexible, and it's time for companies to fully embrace this shift. Flexibility is not just a perk or a temporary solution; it's a fundamental change in how we approach work. By prioritizing flexibility, autonomy, and work-life integration, companies can create a more humane workplace where employees are empowered to do their best work, without sacrificing their well-being.

This book has explored the many benefits of flexibility, from increased productivity and job satisfaction to improved gender equity and environmental sustainability. But the journey doesn't end here. It's up to HR leaders, managers, and executives to continue advocating for flexible work policies that support both employees and the business.

The key to a successful, flexible workplace is trust—trusting employees to manage their own time, trusting managers to lead with empathy, and trusting that the results will speak for themselves. The future of work is about more than where we work; it's about creating an environment that values people, respects their time, and allows them to thrive.

Let's build that future together.

ABOUT THE AUTHOR

I'm Frederique Bergeron, an HR leader and author who's passionate about creating workplaces that prioritize people, flexibility, and innovation. Over the past 25 years, I've worked with organizations to navigate the challenges of modern work environments, helping them build cultures that are grounded in trust, empathy, and employee engagement.

As an advocate for remote and hybrid work, I've helped businesses implement flexible work models that benefit both employees and companies. My approach is shaped by years of experience in talent management, organizational development, and fostering employee well-being.

In my writing, I focus on how technology, evolving workforce trends, and shifting societal expectations are transforming the way we work. I'm dedicated to exploring the intersection of business, technology, and human connection, and I'm excited to share practical strategies for thriving in a world where work is no longer confined to the office.

I am a certified human resource professional, and when I'm not writing or consulting, you can find me spending time with family and traveling. **"Flex Revolution: Redefining the Future of Work"** is my latest book, and it offers a roadmap for embracing the flexibility and freedom that define the future of work.

www.ingramcontent.com/pod-product-compliance
Lightning Source LLC
Chambersburg PA
CBHW070408230526
45471CB00006B/2705